YACHTS IN COLOR

YACHTS

in Color

BY A. K. BEKEN, F.R.P.S.

A STUDIO BOOK
THE VIKING PRESS, NEW YORK

First published, 1961

LIBRARY OF CONGRESS CATALOG CARD NUMBER: 61–5347

PRINTED AND BOUND IN GREAT BRITAIN BY
JARROLD AND SONS LTD. LONDON AND NORWICH,
FOR THE PUBLISHERS
THE VIKING PRESS
625 MADISON AVENUE, NEW YORK 22, N.Y.

CONTENTS

List of Plates   7

INTRODUCTION   9

    Stretching a Terylene Sail   15

    The Flow in Sails   15

    Keep your Spars straight   17

    Battens   18

    Get off your Boat   19

    Washing Terylene Sails   19

    Mildew and Rot   19

    Washing—special methods   20

THE PLATES   23

THE PLATES

International Star Class	25
World Traveller—*Wanderer III*	27
Black Soo	29
Merry Dancer	31
A Royal Racing Yacht—*Coweslip*	33
Lumberjack	35
The Dancing Debutantes—International One Designs	37
The Spritty Barge—*Five Sisters*	39
Butterflies—the Dragon Class	41
Hamburg VI	43
The International 505 Class	45
Macrimia	47
Vision II	49
Maaslust	51
"Six o'Clock in the Morning"	53
Tawau	55
Sceptre	57
The Hornet Class	59
Drumbeat	61
Creole	63
A New Type—*Fairey Fox*	65
Columbia, the Champion	67
South Coast One Design	69
Summer Idyll	71

INTRODUCTION

During the course of more than thirty years of sailing and photographing yachts, I have come to the conclusion that a sailing ship rarely fails to capture the eye and imagination of the would-be yachtsman, professional or amateur, and even of the landlubber. This is not surprising because of the inherent beauty and excitement of a ship under sail. Nothing can compare with the sweeping lines, the grace and the majesty of a yacht in motion.

Yachting is as popular today as it was in the years preceding World War II, and small boats are even more popular.

The sailing dinghy, of which the Hornet and International 505 Class illustrated are typical, is now universally used. Fifty years ago the racing dinghy, as such, was unknown. The youngster then in his teens graduated from a rowing boat to a keel yacht and thereby missed the delights of dinghy racing, with all its thrills and action. Racing dinghies vary from the smallest size, about 9 feet in length, to 18 feet. They are in effect 'open boats', can be handled by one or two persons, and are designed for 'class' racing, which is perhaps the most exciting racing, as close tactics are employed, giving the youngster a chance to use his knowledge and imagination to gain the coveted first place 'gun'.

The youth of today are sailing dinghies almost as soon as they can walk—a fine thing for their health. Dinghy racing teaches them also to be independent and to fight the elements of wind and water. And what finer upbringing in the world of sport could children have?

After the dinghy-type yacht comes the keel yacht, with its fixed keel; either the fin-and-bulb type or the built-in keel. The Star is a typical class in which the yacht has an iron plate fixed to the bottom of the hull and a heavy bulbous keel below. These yachts are decked in, and they are fast and exciting. Used strictly for racing, they have a large sail area which gives them speed and makes sailing them a thrilling experience. In Europe and especially in America they are extremely popular, and to see the crews leaning far over the gunwale, 'sitting them out', makes one realize how fit they have to be to sail these craft.

The Flying Fifteen, illustrated by *Coweslip*, another fin-and-bulb keel boat, was designed by Uffa Fox, to fill a gap between the racing dinghy and the deep-keel yacht. These yachts are well decked in, can go out in most weathers and are great fun to race. They have just one forestay and two mainstays, and no runners, but carry a permanent backstay. They plane at the slightest excuse and give more comfort to the helmsman and crew as they have a wide deck on which one can sit, hooking one's feet under toe-straps for support.

The Dragon Class, of Scandinavian design, is a two- or three-man racing yacht of world renown. These tough little boats, originally designed by Johan Anker as cruiser-racers, are out-and-out racing machines. They measure just over 29 feet in overall length and 18 feet 6 inches on the waterline, with a beam of 6 feet 4 inches and a draught of 4 feet. They carry a sail area of about 250 square feet.

Next in size is the 5½-metre yacht of Olympic standards, and her larger and less expensive sister class, the International One Design. The 5½-metre class has almost taken the place of the more expensive 6-metre class, raced by a crew of three. The class is not strictly of one design. The rules say, basically, that if you increase the sail area you have to make the boat smaller and vice versa. This allows the designer some latitude to prove his skill and judgement in the designing of the fastest 5½-metre he can produce.

The International One Design class is strictly of one design, and very little latitude is given to the designer. Thus, even more than usual it is up to the dexterity of the helmsman and crew to win first place. This class has more room inboard, with a useful cabin as shelter for crew and storage of sails.

The last of the out-and-out racing yachts illustrated in this book are the 12-metre class yachts, *Sceptre* of Great Britain, and *Columbia* of America.

12-metre yachts were originally built as cruising vessels, suitable for hard racing in almost any conditions. This has given way to the modern light-displacement types which are now being produced. Typical dimensions for these craft are an overall length of about 70 feet with a waterline length of 45 feet—beam about 11 feet 6 inches and draught 8–9 feet.

Sceptre, the last challenger for the *America*'s Cup, was designed by

David Boyd of Scotland. The yacht created great interest for she had a deep well-deck from which practically the whole crew worked. All winches and the handling of sails were controlled from there. Great speculation was caused by her use of the huge French-designed 'Herbulot' spinnaker which is shown in the illustration.

Columbia, the defender, is shown in the *America*'s Cup races with her spinnaker flying high and pulling her to victory. She was designed in America by Olin Stephens, and, considering the limits of the 12-metre class, the difference in hull form between her and *Sceptre* is remarkable. *Columbia*, stripped of all expendable gear, is probably the fastest sailing vessel in the world of the type she represents. All her sails were made of Terylene with the exception of the spinnaker, as were all sheets, a portent of the future when man-made fibres will have taken the place of natural fibres.

The next stage in yachting brings us to the cruiser-racer type of yacht. These, as their name implies, are used for both cruising and racing. The South Coast One Design class, designed by Charles Nicholson of England, has filled a long-felt need for a fast, moderately priced, strongly built boat, with good accommodation. As such, they are extremely popular.

The ocean racer, or cruiser, can be of unlimited size, as the photographs of *Black Soo*, *Drumbeat*, and *Hamburg VI* show. In races, these yachts are handicapped according to waterline length, sail area carried, draught and a number of other measurements which when put together give their

12

T.C.F. (Time Correction Factor). The designs of these craft are as varied as their sizes: *Hamburg VI* was designed by Stevens of America, *Drumbeat* by Ray Hunt of America, *Merry Dancer* by Fife of Scotland. Each of them was built for ocean racing, to accommodate their crews in comfort, and to withstand the worst weather conditions that the elements can produce.

A description of the building of these yachts, the materials used and the methods of application could alone fill many thousands of pages. Wood is, of course, the traditional boat-building material; steel, aluminium and, now, glass fibre are also extensively used.

There is no reason why a well-built yacht of wood should not last *at least* thirty years if it is well looked after and maintained. White oak and teak are the woods in most general use, and since it is known that they do not decay in salt water, the raw wood is immersed in it and allowed to season, sometimes up to twenty years or more before a boat is built. Salt-water seasoning produces a very tough and long-lasting timber. Other ways of protecting timber against rot include the use of chemicals, and, by using the best material available, a yacht owner today can keep his maintenance down to a minimum.

Plywood, with its several thin layers of various thicknesses of wood glued together, has now revolutionized the building of yacht hulls. Equal strength with less weight is attained as a result of its use. Glues have improved so much over the past ten years that the plywood hull is virtually impervious to separation or attack by worm.

Yachts can be built by using laminated plywood strips, moulded plywood, or sheet plywood. Where, originally, natural-shaped pieces of oak or teak were used for stem, keel and stern-posts, laminated plywood, of any required thickness, is now extensively employed, and is as tough and resistant as natural wood. Many lifeboats now have laminated wood for stem, keel, dead-wood and stern-post, all very often being laminated in one piece. Flaws that may occur in a stem of natural wood might never be seen; in laminated wood there can be no flaws. Furthermore, metal fastenings are kept to a minimum in laminated framing.

Moulded plywood, which is now coming into prominence in boat construction, is moulded over an original shape. No framing is required in these hulls, and the interior is naturally smooth and clean. High-speed launches and racing dinghies are now made this way, and, as a result, have light-weight hulls, combined with great strength. Sheet plywood is also popular in building hard-chine hulls, of great strength, with the use of up-to-date waterproof glues.

Glass-fibre hulls are greatly on the increase, particularly in America where it is said that 90 per cent of the small yachts are built of some form of glass fibre. The advantages of this material are many: there is no water absorption and no painting is necessary (the colour being mixed into the original resins), the product is impervious to worm and any damage can easily be repaired by untrained labour. Fittings, such as seats and instrument panels, can also be made of glass fibre.

Next let us examine sails. The finest sails ever made can be ruined through neglect and improper handling. The following instructions are those of the famous firm of Ratsey & Lapthorn of Cowes and New York.

STRETCHING A TERYLENE SAIL

This is much simpler than stretching a cotton sail. It does not matter whether it rains or snows, and only an hour or two of sailing in any reasonable weight of wind should see the sail near its mark, and ready to race or cruise. The same general principles, however, apply as with a cotton sail: pull your sail well out until the wrinkles disappear, and don't sheet the sail in until it is near its mark and setting well.

THE FLOW IN SAILS

As all sailors know, the most effective form of sail is one which is curved like a bird's wing: the forward section of the sail has a distinct curve, or flow, which gradually flattens towards the middle of the sail, ending in a practically flat surface in the region of the leech, or after edge. It is not unlike the carefully constructed curve in the wing of a modern aeroplane. In fact an aeroplane wing, 'mounted on end' in a small boat, has been made to propel the boat to windward.

In a Marconi or jib-headed sail, the draught, or flow, is kept in the forward part of the sail by setting up on the halyard so that there is more strain on the luff-rope than there is on the foot-rope.

The draught can be moved aft to a certain extent, by slacking off a little on the halyard and pulling out on the outhaul. Conversely, it can be moved forward by increased tension on the halyard and less on the outhaul.

In a gaff-headed sail the draught, or flow, is obtained by pulling out the head of the sail along the gaff until some strain comes on the canvas. This strain is widened by the appearance of small wrinkles or folds running parallel to the head rope; then the sail is set, head to wind, luff-rope properly taut, and gaff 'peaked up,' until small wrinkles or folds appear running from the peak, or gaff end, to the tack of the sail.

After a period of time, depending on weather conditions and on the amount of stretch allowed by the sailmaker, the head of the sail may stretch beyond the available length of the gaff. Then it should either be re-roped or have a piece cut from it, whichever the sailmaker decides is best for the sail. The same treatment is called for on the foot of the sail, should it stretch beyond the limit established by the boom end.

If the head of the sail is too long for the gaff, the draught or flow in the sail will be too far aft—too near the middle section of the sail—a defect generally considered fatal for speed to windward. No amount of 'peaking up' the gaff will help matters.

If the foot of either a gaff or Marconi sail is too long for the boom, the sail cannot be flattened out as much as it should be, but this will not cause the draught to come too far back in the sail.

KEEP YOUR SPARS STRAIGHT

If any sail, properly cut by a competent sailmaker, is designed and built to set on straight spars, common sense suggests that it will not set well if the spars bend or buckle when the yacht is under way. Spars which are quite straight when the boat is swinging idly at her moorings may take on some unexpected and remarkable curves when she is being sailed in a good breeze.

Anyone at the helm is in a poor position to determine whether or not his spars are buckling, and if so how much and in what direction.

If you have a companion sailor on board you can find out if the boom is buckling by going forward while he is sailing the boat to windward in a smart breeze, and glancing along the boom with your eye close to the gooseneck, much as you would sight a rifle. You will probably be amazed to see that the boom, which you thought quite straight, has taken on quite a curve. The remedy lies in re-arranging main-sheet leads, or bridles, to bring the strain in the right place to cure the buckling. If this treatment is ineffective, probably your boom is too small in diameter, or just too limber.

Now go forward, lie down on deck, and glance along the mast. Curves and buckles? Possibly. Careful adjustment of headstays, shrouds, and backstays is necessary to cure the 'bends' in a mast. Occasionally, a limber mast will have to be replaced by a stiffer one. Or perhaps rigging and spreaders are not placed properly on the mast. In case of extreme difficulty with either mast or boom, call in an expert. But at all costs keep your spars straight if you expect your sails to set properly.

Spars are usually tapered, well-made ones on the side opposite to that on which the sail is attached: the forward side of the mast and underside of the boom. Therefore, when 'sighting' spars, see that the after or 'track' side of the mast is in a straight line, not the fore side; the top of the boom should be straight, not the underside.

This of course applies only to sails designed to set on straight spars. In a large number of small boats, sails are meant to be used on spars that will bend a certain amount so as to flatten the sail somewhat in strong winds. In fact it is probably true to say that on most dinghies, and on many other small boats as well, masts do bend to a certain degree, and it is not only helpful, but essential, for the sailmaker to know to what extent the spars will bend.

BATTENS

The question of wood versus plastic for battens is often argued at length. However, wood is still preferred. Hickory is the best and almost only suitable kind; it is lighter than plastic and the batten can be tapered correctly. Battens should have two coats of varnish otherwise they may warp when wet.

Have your battens an inch or so shorter than the pockets in which they fit. If they are too long they will wear a hole in the inboard end of the pocket, or through the body of the sail itself. For lighter weather it is a good idea to have a more flexible top batten than usual.

GET OFF YOUR BOAT

In order to determine the set of your sails, and the proper lead and trim of sheets, it is advisable to get aboard another craft while someone else sails your boat. You will see things which are in no way apparent when you are aboard your own craft. Take a good, long look, from all angles. Although you can see many things from your own cockpit, nevertheless 'see your sails as others see them'. Your time will be well spent.

WASHING TERYLENE SAILS

Terylene sails can be washed in the normal fashion, using a soap or soda solution or solution of any brand of detergent, as hot as the hand can bear.

For persistent stains, scrub *lightly* with the solution. Soaking overnight in a 10 per cent solution of sodium metasilicate, followed by a normal wash, may also prove beneficial.

MILDEW AND ROT

Never furl a wet sail. If you do, you are simply inviting mildew and rot. Bundle it up loosely so the air can get to it.

The worst possible treatment for a damp or wet sail is to furl it tight and let the sun beat down on the outside; and steam, mildew, and rot will go to work on the inside. Air out wet sails at the first possible moment. In light weather, hoist your sails, moderately taut only on the luff, head, and foot, and let the water drain off, so that the dry atmosphere can get at the entire sail at the same time.

When drying sails, remember that the corners, because of the several thicknesses of canvas reinforcing at these points, take much longer to dry out than the body of the sail. The same is usually true of the roping along the edges. Never pull hard on a damp luff-rope or foot-rope: let them stretch out naturally to their previous length, which they will do as they dry, if you will give them time. Although mildew has been known to form on Terylene, it is very rare. The producers have informed us that Terylene is not affected by mildew.

WASHING—SPECIAL METHODS

In each case, these suggestions refer only to white materials. Coloured sails which become abnormally stained should be dealt with by an experienced finisher or dry cleaner.

Mildew. Scrub *lightly* when dry to remove as *much* of the stain as possible, then steep the affected areas for $1\frac{1}{2}$ hours at room temperature in a solution containing one part of sodium bisulphite to a thousand parts of water, and wash again.

Oil. Lubricating oil is seldom clean but liable to be contaminated with dirt and finely divided metal such as copper, bronze, or steel. Fuel oils and bunker residues may contain bituminous substances, which can be very difficult to remove, but which sometimes yield to solvent treatment.

Always try to avoid rubbing the oil into the interstices of the fabric. While the stains are dry, dab them with a solvent such as carbon tetrachloride or trichlorethylene or a detergent such as Stergene. The latter, if thoroughly mixed with the oil, will make it self-emulsifying on subsequent washing in warm water.

Vigorous flexing should be used. If the oil is too thick to mix with the detergent, it may be helpful to mix one part of a concentrated detergent with two parts of a solvent, and apply with a paint brush, working the mixture well in. Any remaining stain is probably a metallic solid which can be removed with oxalic or hydrofluoric acid.

These operations should be carried out in a well-ventilated space as some of the reagents are inflammable and all are somewhat toxic. Contact with the skin should also be avoided.

Paint. Paint stains should yield to a solvent based on paint stripper. Do not use an alkali-based stripper. Wash well afterwards.

Stainless Steel. Pour a 10 per cent solution of hot oxalic acid on to the fabric and allow it to permeate slowly and dissolve the deposit. For small deposits, sponge with a warm solution for a few minutes, treat with ammonia to neutralize and then wash thoroughly. Oxalic acid is poisonous, so care should be used in handling it.

Tar. Solvent naphtha, white spirit or turpentine should prove successful and certain proprietary cleansing agents recommended for this purpose may also be effective.

THE PLATES

International Star Class

The Stars are world renowned. Fast, full of action, with a large sail area, they provide an inexhaustible amount of pleasure.
Spain, Portugal, America, Germany, Scandinavia, the Mediterranean—they are everywhere, and they are of Olympic standards. Here we see two lads, like Red Indian horsemen slung side-saddle, urging every ounce of power out of the boat, to winkle her up to windward.

World Traveller

Round the world—not in eighty days, but in a more leisurely and enjoyable fashion. Here is *Wanderer III* owned by Eric Hiscock and his wife: a pretty and practical yacht with just the necessary amount of rigging of the right standard, first-class design and well sailed by a master of the art of sailing. She is 30 feet overall, 26 feet on the waterline with a draught of 5 feet.

Black Soo

This intrepid little ocean racer, *Black Soo*, is travelling at her best under spinnaker and main. Hard-chine with a fin-and-bulb keel, she is an exhilarating yacht to sail. Designed by E. Van de Stadt of Holland, she has many novel features. Her fin and keel are made of iron, hollowed and filled with lead. In bad weather she can be helmed from inside the cabin; she has a Perspex cabin top through which the helmsman can see. She will plane like a dinghy in rough weather, and has taken part in races under the toughest weather conditions.

28

Merry Dancer

Using every ounce of power, *Merry Dancer* flies for the open sea. Rolling cumulus clouds above and a blue sea beneath, this picture is typical of yachting at its best.

A Royal Racing Yacht

Coweslip is a Flying Fifteen designed, and here seen raced, by Uffa Fox. She was presented to H.R.H. The Duke of Edinburgh by the people of Cowes. A slim keel-boat, in a very popular class, a joy to race in weather fair or foul. She has the feel of a larger yacht and retains all the zest of an international dinghy.

This little racing yacht planes on the slightest excuse, has more comfort than a dinghy, and is sailed with ease.

32

Lumberjack

     This very attractive yacht designed by de Vries Lentsch of Holland was originally called *Norbar* and is built of steel. Known as a staysail schooner, she has an interesting rig, in deteriorating weather she can shorten sail very quickly and easily, and can remain well balanced even when reduced to an absolute minimum of sail area.

In this picture she is carrying a Genoa, fisherman's staysail, main foresail and mainsail.

34

The Dancing Debutantes

These International One Designs are of Scandinavian origin, and
their numbers have increased by leaps and bounds, both in Scandinavia
and in England. They are an ideal day racer, fast and powerful and,
with a cabin below, make an ideal day cruiser. This class has filled a
gap between the 6-metre class and the Dragon class in both size and cost.

36

The Spritty Barge

What a lovely sight on a lovely day! *Five Sisters*, as she is called, is one of the few remaining barge yachts. Oceans of cabin space, with plenty of room for a 'grand piano', they are extremely popular, and consequently are at a premium. Here *Five Sisters* is slipping quietly but by no means slowly down the Solent bound for the open channel.

38

Butterflies

The Dragon class of international fame increases from year to year. Of Scandinavian design, these boats are built the world over and compete in the Olympic races. Built and tuned as delicately as any violin, they spread their wings on lakes, rivers and the open sea. Here we see *Chow* sliding away from her competitors for the next mark. The Dragons weigh 4 tons and are 29 feet overall in length.

Hamburg VI

This fine German yacht is a typical ocean racer first class. With spinnaker set round to leeward, her mizzen staysail set to perfection, she uses every stitch of her canvas to produce her maximum speed. The crew are watching points, and there are plenty of points to watch in a yacht like this. 'How's the mast standing the strain? Can we ease that spinnaker an inch? Can we point a fraction higher?' A picture of bright varnished teak and green seas.

42

The International 505 Class

This class is of reasonably recent date and has leaped into prominence as a most practical and exciting dinghy to race.
Large numbers have been built in England and France. They are well decked in and comfortable. Trapezes can be used by the crew to enable them to sit well out to windward. They are virtually unsinkable and if they capsize can be quickly righted, and sailed on, the water escaping through scuppers in the transom.

44

Macrimia

This yacht, of a type extremely popular in France, is a typical motor sailer. There is enough power below to give her a cruising speed of about 12 knots, plenty of accommodation and a good sail area to send her along at a cracking pace, as seen in the picture.

She was designed by a French architect, M. Cornu, and built at Deauville. Her overall length is about 53 feet and she carries 1,000 square feet of canvas.

46

Vision II

The 5½-metre class yacht *Vision II* was designed by Arthur Robb of England. The class is an Olympic class and is increasing fast in popularity. With her new Terylene mainsail and huge nylon spinnaker she is tuning up for possible Olympic races.

48

Maaslust

    Maaslust is a type of yacht seen on so many of Holland's water-ways. Of steel construction with leeboards for shallow waters and plenty of room below, she is many a yachtsman's dream. *Maaslust* travelled far and wide. She took part in the epic Dunkirk evacuation, during the Second World War, and ended her days in a fierce gale in the English Channel, fortunately without loss of life.

50

"Six o'Clock in the Morning"

This is a sight seen by relatively few people. Six o'clock in the morning and a rising sun tipping the hulls of the closely nestled yachts. Crews below decks are stretching their limbs before another day's hard racing, for a strong westerly breeze is forecast, giving the lie to this pleasant early morning calm.

Ocean racers, international dinghies, cruisers, all are here waiting for their owners to ready them for another day's delight.

52

Tawau

What a fine old-timer! Or perhaps not so old, as she was built in 1929 and there are many far older.

With main reefed, and two headsails plus a mizzen, she threshes her way comfortably to windward, spurning all seas and torments the elements can produce.

Tawau is 74 feet overall, with a waterline length of 50 feet, and she carries nearly 3,000 square feet of canvas.

54

Sceptre

The 12-metre yacht *Sceptre* is seen here with her huge French spinnaker designed by M. Herbulot. She was the unsuccessful challenger for the *America*'s Cup in 1958.

The 12-metre class is the finest example of the modern racing yacht. Stripped of every unnecessary gadget, weight down to a minimum, tall spars with as little rigging as possible, she races as smoothly and swiftly as a greyhound round a track.

56

The Hornet

A now very popular class of hard-chine dinghy, particularly favoured by the younger sailing enthusiasts. In this photograph she is shown with a sliding seat, which enables the crew to sit outside the hull. With this added leverage the hull can easily be kept on an even keel.

Striped sails are now increasing in popularity and add a touch of colour to the usual white sails and green sea. This one has a Terylene mainsail and foresail, and a nylon spinnaker.

58

Drumbeat

Designed by Ray Hunt of America, *Drumbeat* runs smartly under main, foresail and staysail. This very fine ocean racer has twin centreboards, set side by side, which when raised allow her to run like a stag from the rest of the class.

She has twice raced in the Newport–Bermuda race and has sailed across the Atlantic. With her varnished teak hull and white Terylene sails she will capture the imagination of any onlooker.

60

Creole

   A beautiful three-masted staysail schooner coasting along with a brand-new spinnaker just set by an anxious crew.

This tremendous spinnaker of nearly 9,000 square feet, the spinnaker boom nearly 61 feet long, fascinates the crew of cadets who are sailing her.

Creole, designed by the late Charles E. Nicholson, is nearly 200 feet overall and has a working sail area of 17,000 square feet.

A New Type

Fairey Fox, as she is called, heels and leaps forward in urgency. With Uffa Fox at her helm, this 24-foot open boat races almost as a dinghy. She is a centreboard boat, has a gaff mainsail which can be easily reefed and can plane when the winds demand.

Notice in the stern the two outlets for water taken aboard in a race. The boat has a 7-foot beam and draws only 1 foot. She was designed by Uffa Fox, and is owned by H.R.H. The Duke of Edinburgh.

64

Columbia, the Champion

This picture of *Columbia*, the successful *America*'s Cup defender, shows her with her nylon spinnaker flying high, pulling her to victory in the *America*'s Cup Races of 1958.

Every detail of this 12-metre points to a thoroughbred. With every rope and sail of the finest materials, and an enviable hull, she beat her challenger *Sceptre* with minutes to spare. Designed by Olin Stephens of America, and sailed by Briggs Cunningham, she portrays everything that is worthy of a champion.

South Coast One Design

A small channel cruiser-racer at moderate cost, to sleep four: the day sailer, the week-end cruiser, the ideal boat for a month's holiday, or a race round the buoys.

This sturdy little craft, designed by C. Nicholson, is of 6 tons and is 26 feet overall, fast and comfortable. The class is fast gaining popularity.

Summer Idyll

A can of iced lager in one hand, a chicken leg in the other, one foot on the wheel, and snatches of conversation drifting from the other yachts. Those who have known this will appreciate it, those who have not have missed a great experience.

With reflections dropping great blobs of moving colour at your feet, this is a peaceful scene amidst a noisy world.